ROBOTS

Kathy Galashan

Published in association with The Basic Skills Agency

Hodder & Stoughton

A MEM

Acknowledgements
Cover: © Haruyoshi Yamaguchi/Corbis Sygma

Photos: pp. 2, 12 © Tony Kyriacou/Rex Features; pp. 4, 23 © BFI Stills, Posters and
Designs; p. 9 © NASA/Roger Ressmeyer/CORBIS; p. 18 © PA Photos.

Every effort has been made to trace copyright holders of material reproduced in this book.
Any rights not acknowledged will be acknowledged in subsequent printings if notice is
given to the publisher.

Basic Skills
Collection

Orders; please contact Bookpoint Ltd, 130 Milton Park, Abingdon, Oxon OX14 4SB.
Telephone (44) 01235 827720, Fax: (44) 01235 400454. Lines are open from 9.00–6.00,
Monday to Saturday, with a 24 hour message answering service.
You can also order through our website www.hodderheadline.co.uk

British Library Cataloguing in Publication Data
A catalogue record for this title is available from the British Library

ISBN 0 340 87311 6

First published 2003
Impression number   10 9 8 7 6 5 4 3 2 1
Year   2009 2008 2007 2006 2005 2004 2003

Copyright © Kathy Galashan 2003

Typeset by SX Composing DTP, Rayleigh, Essex.
Printed in Great Britain for Hodder & Stoughton Educational, a division of Hodder
Headline, 338 Euston Road, London NW1 3BH by Bath Press Ltd, Bath.

Contents

1 What is a Robot?

Why make robots?
Can a robot think?
What can a robot do?
How does a robot work?
Read on and find out.

A robot is a machine
that can do all sorts of things.
It is run by a computer programme.
A robot is different to other machines
because it can do things on its own.

Many robots can make choices.
The choices depend on the programs.
First you think of the job
you want the robot to do.
Then you program it.

A robot at the Science Museum in London.

Think of the robots in the TV programme,
Robot Wars.
What about R2D2 in *Star Wars*?
Are these <u>true</u> robots?
Well, they are controlled by people.
They can't work by themselves.
They don't make choices.
They are controlled by someone off-stage.

Star Wars robots, R2D2 and C3PO.

2 Why Make Robots?

This is a very exciting time for robotmakers.
There seems to be no end of things robots can do.

Robots in industry.
Robots are great in factories.
They don't need a break.
They don't make mistakes
and they don't argue.
They don't get tired
and they can keep working for hours.
They keep doing the same thing
over and over again.
They never ask for more money
or come in late.
A robot is an ideal worker.

Robots making cars at the Ford factory.

Robots as explorers.

Robots are used in places where it is
dangerous for people to go.
They can check cables on the sea floor.
They can explore the surface of the moon.

They are used to check on volcanoes.
Is a volcano going to explode?
Do people need to leave the area?

They have been used to explore
the future and the past.
Robots were sent into the pyramids in Egypt.
They found a new room.

How can you clear a poison dump?
What about a nuclear disaster?
Robots can work when it is very hot and very cold.
They don't need clean air.
They can work deep underground or underwater.

Think of other places where people can't go
and where robots could be used.

An astronaut using a robotic arm to repair the Hubble Space Telescope.

Robots as servants.
Do you want a robot guard dog
or a robot security guard?

Very soon there will be one on the market.
The robotic patrolman can patrol
a building at 3km an hour.
It can go into lifts.
It can warn people of a fire
or of someone breaking in.
It could act on that warning.

But suppose it was wrong.
Suppose the person is a young child,
in the wrong place at the wrong time.
If something goes wrong,
do you blame the robot,
the maker or the owner?

Robots as pets.
AIBO is a robot dog.
They were put on the market in 1999.
In 20 minutes, they were sold out.
In total, 3,000 dogs were sold.

The dog can understand commands.
It will do what you say.
You can play with it.
The dog can be happy, angry or sad.
It's a robot pet.

An AIBO robodog.

3   What Makes a Robot Work?

A robot is like a person.
It finds out what is going on around it.
Then it decides what to do about it.
It picks up information from the outside.
Then what it does changes.

A person finds out about the world
through their senses.
We can hear, see, touch, smell and feel.
A robot needs to do the same.
Some are sensitive to sound.
Others are sensitive to touch.
Some can check out electric currents.

Sensors are built into robots.
The sensors read what is going on
in the outside world.
The information is fed into a computer.
The computer programme decides
what the robot will do.

Let's take a robot servant.
The robot is programmed to look after the house.
The programme can be a set of rules.

1. Open the door when the bell rings.

That's easy.
Or

2. Open the door if it is Mary

That's easy too.
It can check fingerprints or photos.
Or

3. Open the door if it is a girl.

That's difficult.

How will the computer know
it is a girl rather than a boy?
What sensors can tell the difference?
The sensors can look for clues,
such as less body hair and breasts.
The robot can make a good guess,
but it can make mistakes.

Some robots can learn from mistakes.
They can learn that girls may have short hair.
Girls can be big or small.

It may be that voices give the best clues.
What they learn can feed back
into the program
and help make better guesses.

So can a robot think?
Can a robot act like a person?
That is the challenge for scientists.
There is a whole field of study called
artificial intelligence.
This tries to work out
how people's brains work
and how to make robots think.

4 Setting a Challenge

Can you talk to a robot
and think it is a person?
Or can you always tell
you are talking to a machine?

This is a hard challenge
because we use words
in many different ways.

Up to now no computer has tricked
a person in a long conversation.
It's OK to begin with,
but then the chat
stops making sense.

5 Robot Football

Robotmakers set themselves a problem.
As they look for answers
they build different, better robots.
Robotmakers all over the world
compete in robot cup football.
Twelve teams took part in RoboCup 2002.

Think of all the problems
a robot football player faces.

It must move round the pitch.
It has to know where the other players are
and where the ball is.
It has to score goals or defend the goal.
It has to work in a team.

The winning team is the one
that solves these problems best.
Could you have a robot football manager?
Can a robot plan strategies?
That is another challenge.

The opening match of RoboCup 2002.

6 The Future

Robots already do many things
We never dreamed possible.
They conduct operations on people.
They have explored outer space.

At the moment they are not common.
Many people have never seen a real robot.
In the future, there could be one in homes,
in schools and at work.
Once robots are cheaper to make
then we will start using them.
They will be part of our everyday lives.

What jobs would you like a robot to do?
Could it help with homework,
or run a business?
Could it cut the grass or weed the garden?
Could it run a dating agency?

Perhaps, one day, there will be
a robot colony in space.
Robots could make other robots.
These could work in teams
to build and develop a space station.
Is it possible?
Why not?

Imagine a robot controlled
by your own brain.
A robot controlled by your mind.
You could think a robot through a job
and it could do it.

This is also the future.

7 What Can People Do That Robots Can't?

Your brain can think in different ways.
It can come up with something new.

Maybe you can write a new song.
Perhaps a robot can also do that.
You can create a new sound,
like jazz, pop or hip hop.

Music, art, fun, films, cooking.
You bring new ideas to what you do every day.
No robot can come up with an original idea.

In a factory a robot follows rules.
What happens if things change?
Then you need people to decide things.

Can a robot come up with a new idea?
You can imagine a car
that runs on sunlight or electricity.
Can a robot do that?

You can think and feel.
What you do depends
on what you think and feel.
You can even think about
what you think and feel.

Imagine you are hungry.
It's time for food.
Then you remember you are on a diet.
Yesterday you didn't eat much.
Today is your birthday.
Your friend says you look great.
So you think about all these things
and then decide what to eat.

Is this what makes people and robots different?
One thing is for sure.
Learning about robots shows us
how amazing WE are.

Haley Joel Osment as the robot boy in the film *A.I.*

Can robots take over the world or outer space?
Can they take control?
They can only follow a program.
They cannot create new ones.
So they can't take control.

Can they be dangerous?
Well that depends on the program.
It depends on the people
behind the program.
A good program would stop
robots making trouble.

If there are problems,
it is with people not machines.
Robots are not good or bad in themselves.
It is how they are used.
Do we want the best for the planet?
Are we clever enough
to manage our inventions?

Only the future will tell.

8 Glossary

Alien	Something or person from outer space.
Animatronics	The study of moving models and toys.
Artificial Intelligence	The study of how people think and how to make thinking machines.
Automata	An automated toy that looks like a person or creature.
Automated Toy	A toy which moves by switches and controls. The controls can be radio or electronic.
Dating Agency	A way to find a partner for fun or love.
Invention	A new idea.
Jazz, Pop, Hip Hop	Three different sorts of music.

Robot Wars	A TV series. Homemade robots battle against each other to win a competition.
RoboCup	A football league for robot teams.
Sensor	A sensor measures what is going on around it. Different sensors measure different things.